North Pole Marketing

Santa's Secrets for Successful Marketing, Fulfillment and Customer Service

*Who else except Santa Claus
has had a successful business
for more than 1,400 years*

As told to
John M. Chilson
by
Santa Claus

Dedicated to the many people who mentored, nurtured, guided and encouraged me in the fun sport of Marketing and Customer Service. Named here are just a few but there were many others: Dan Bench, Earl Hogan, Lee Pierce, Joel Champion, Mike Branch, Terri Smith, Chris Lynde, Matt York, Audrey Miller, Mike Deardorff, Mike Harvey, Pari Rickard, Mike Riester, Barry Smith and Bruce Barrell.

North Pole Marketing

Introduction

Several years ago I had an opportunity to spend some time with Santa Claus. As we talked, he shared with me his secrets for Marketing, Fulfillment and Customer Service, which he developed and has used over the past 1,400 years.

This book contains 52 of Santa's secrets. Each has a suggestion on how it can be applied to your organization.

I hope this little book will encourage you to do things you have never done before and help you breathe new life into your organization.

With 52 of Santa's secrets, why not focus on one a week? In a year you may have a very different organization.

During that year, don't be afraid to shake things up.

For more information, or to contact either Santa or me, please visit our internet web site at www.NorthPoleMarketing.com.

John M. Chilson

If you do what you've always done, you'll get what you've always gotten.

Anthony Robbins
Self–help Author
and Success Coach

Not a shred of evidence exists in favor of the idea that life is serious.

Brendan Gill
Writer for
The New Yorker
for over 60 years

North Pole Marketing

List of Santa's Secrets

1. All children are alike
2. Each child is different
3. Children change every year
4. Make your list, check it twice
5. Stay in touch
6. Manage expectations
7. Play with the toys
8. Don't forget to fill the stockings
9. Learn from your mistakes
10. Exceed children's expectations
11. Make children happy
12. Go the extra mile
13. It was Rudolph's idea
14. Consider alternatives
15. Santa needs to be seen
16. Watch the weather
17. Plan early, change quickly
18. The Easter Bunny is *not* competition
19. Update the flight plan every year
20. Test, test, test
21. *OOPS!*
22. Santa is recognized *instantly*
23. Keep the elves happy
24. Don't eat too many cookies
25. Remember what you will ALWAYS do
26. Remember what you will NEVER do
27. Set the criteria for all toys

North Pole Marketing

28. Bookkeepers don't deliver presents
29. Remember your FIRST priority
30. Santa always delivers
31. If it is broken, fix it
32. If it is not broken, change it
33. Say "Yes" before you say "No"
34. Remember your two basic functions
35. Children can always write to Santa
36. Smile a lot
37. Good elves are made, not born
38. Be positive
39. Show children you can be trusted
40. Speak the child's language
41. Not all children believe in Santa
42. Soften your voice
43. Be dependable
44. Guard each child's privacy
45. If the toy doesn't work, don't wrap it
46. Concentrate on the children
47. Be prepared for a mess
48. Everyone knows what Santa does
49. January is special
50. Take care of the reindeer
51. Don't overload Santa's bag
52. Take time for hot chocolate

1.   All children are alike

Children always want food, warmth, shelter, to be loved and encouraged, and to feel safe and special.

How are your customers alike?

2. Each child is different

*Some want dolls,
others want trucks;
some want a book,
others want building
blocks; some want
electronic toys,
others want a horse.*

How are your
customers different?

3. Children change every year

Eight–year olds don't want the same toys as when they were 7.

How and why do your customers change over time?

4.   Make your list, check it twice

Last year's child on the Naughty List may be on this year's Nice List or vice–versa and they may have moved.

How has your customer base changed in the past year?

5. Stay in touch

Santa is never too busy to talk to the children and he reads all their letters.

Can your customers *easily* get in touch with someone who can change things?

6.   Manage expectations

Santa never promises to deliver anything that won't fit in the sleigh.

Be sure that what you sell is what you can deliver.

7. Play with the toys

Santa plays with all the toys so that he knows they are fun, safe and don't break easily. Besides, he enjoys it.

Does the boss play with your products?

8. Don't forget to fill the stockings

Just putting presents under the Christmas tree is not enough.

What *extras* can you provide to excite your customers?

9. Learn from your mistakes

Before reindeer, Santa tried elephants. They flew well but landing on a housetop was a disaster.

Are you willing to stick your neck out and try something different, even if it may fail?

10. Exceed children's expectations

Children already have high expectations, don't disappoint them. Provide more than they expect.

Are you exceeding your customer's expectations?

11. Make children happy

Santa and his elves will do everything and anything they possibly can to make a child happy.

Is your organization doing all it can to make your customers happy?

12. Go the extra mile

Once in a while Santa flies past a house without delivering the presents. When he realizes his mistake, wherever he is, he immediately turns around and goes back and delivers the presents.

How far and how fast do you go to fix your mistakes?

13. It was Rudolph's idea

All of the other reindeer and Santa thought that Rudolph should not be harnessed in front of the other reindeer. They thought he should fly alongside the sleigh to provide light. They were all wrong.

Is it easy for a low level "hands on" employee to present an idea to the top boss that might improve your business?

14. Consider alternatives

Not all houses have chimneys.

What new or different ways can you use to reach your customers?

North Pole Marketing

15. Santa needs to be seen

Both the elves and the children need to see and talk with Santa and know that everything is under control.

Do your employees and customers ever see and talk to the top boss?

16. Watch the weather

A big storm can seriously delay delivery on Christmas Eve. Thank goodness for Rudolph.

What can seriously mess up your organization, products and delivery and how can you handle it?

17. Plan early, change quickly

Start exercising the reindeer in February but be prepared if Dasher goes lame on December 23rd.

Do you have a "Plan B"?

18. The Easter Bunny is *not* competition

Santa and the Easter Bunny serve the same age group but they are friends, not competitors. They have great respect for each other and often exchange ideas.

Does your organization show respect for others serving the same market? What can you learn from them?

19. Update the flight plan every year

Santa's flight plan for Christmas Eve involves many, many trips back and forth to the North Pole to pick up more presents. Even a small savings in flying time helps everyone involved.

How often do you update your flight (strategic) plan?

20. Test, test, test

Last year's hot toys may not be so hot this year.

Are you checking your market or simply selling the same old thing?

21.   *OOPS!*

Everyone makes mistakes, even Santa and the elves. But they immediately admit it to everyone involved and do their best to fix it quickly, regardless of the cost, time or work involved.

Do you quickly admit and fix your mistakes?

22. Santa is recognized *instantly*

Santa with his white beard and in his red suit is recognized wherever he goes.

Do your customers easily and quickly recognize your products?

23.   Keep the elves happy

Happy elves build better toys.

Are your employees happy?

24. Don't eat too many cookies

If you get too fat you can't get down the chimney.

Are you paying more attention to your organization than your customers?

25. Remember what you will ALWAYS do

There are some things Santa will ALWAYS do — laugh, smile, listen to a child, eat a chocolate chip cookie and be there on Christmas Eve.

What will your organization ALWAYS do?

26. Remember what you will NEVER do

There are some things Santa will NEVER do — lie, break the rules or get upset with a child.

What will your organization NEVER do?

27. Set the criteria for all toys

All toys MUST *fit in the sleigh and go down a chimney.*

Do you design your products with firm criteria from the start?

28. Bookkeepers don't deliver presents

The elves make the presents and Santa delivers them. The bookkeepers simply record what happened.

Do the bookkeepers run your organization?

29. Remember your FIRST priority

Santa's FIRST priority is making children happy. If the procedures don't meet a child's needs, he changes the procedures.

Are your procedures upsetting your customers? How would you know?

30. Santa always delivers

Bobby just moved to a new city. Santa will deliver there instead of to Bobby's old home.

Do you track your customers when they move?

31.   If it is broken, fix it

If what you are doing doesn't work, change it.

What's broken and needs changing in your organization?

32. If it is not broken, change it

If what you are doing works, make it better.

What works, but can be improved, in your organization?

33. Say "Yes" before you say "No"

There are always lots more reasons to say "No", that's why it is important to say "Yes".

Do you say "Yes" or "No" most often to your staff and your customers?

34. Remember your two basic functions

Santa's two basic functions are making children happy and being there for them on Christmas Eve.

What are your organization's two basic functions?

35. Children can always write to Santa

Children write many letters to Santa because they know he reads them.

Do your customers know how to contact you and do they trust that someone will respond?

36.   Smile a lot

Smiling changes the tone of your voice and makes you more friendly and approachable, even on the telephone.

Does everyone in your organization smile a lot?

37. Good elves are made, not born

Elves never stop training.

Do you train, retrain and continue training your employees on how best to do their job?

38.   Be positive

Don't respond to a child or parent's negative comment with your own negative comment. Respond with something positive, helpful and encouraging.

"Thank you for being so patient" is much better than "I'm sorry you had to wait so long". Or "We appreciate you calling this problem to our attention. May we send you a free 'Thank You' gift?"

39. Show children you can be trusted

Although many children run to give Santa a big hug, many approach very slowly until they learn they can trust Santa.

How can you earn the trust of your customers?

40. Speak the child's language

Santa visits children all over the world and always speaks their language.

Do you speak the language of all your customers?

41. Not all children believe in Santa

Unfortunately that is true but Santa still cares for them, respects them and wants to see them happy.

How do you treat people who don't like you, your organization or your products?

42. Soften your voice

A loud booming "Ho Ho Ho" scares many children.

How do you speak to your employees and your customers?

43.   Be dependable

Children all know they can depend on Santa Claus to listen to them, not talk down to them, hug them and be there on Christmas Eve.

How do you show your customers that you are dependable?

44. Guard each child's privacy

Santa and the elves work have a plan in place to protect each child's private information.

Do you have a plan for protecting your customer's private information?

Is it strictly monitored, enforced and regularly updated?

45.   If the toy doesn't work, don't wrap it

It is terrible when a child unwraps a toy that doesn't work.

Do your products always work when the customer receives them?

46. Concentrate on the children

Children are very aware when Santa pays more attention to the adults than to them.

Are you paying attention to your customers?

47. Be prepared for a mess

Some children and elves make a mess but Santa never gets upset.

Do you handle your messes without getting upset?

48. Everyone knows what Santa does

Santa delivers presents on Christmas Eve to children all over the world.

Does everyone know what your organization does?

49. January is special

In January Santa and the elves relax, have fun, review the previous season and plan for the next season.

Does your organization take time to relax, have fun, review and plan?

50. Take care of the reindeer

In order to be healthy and fly all over the world on Christmas Eve, reindeer require lots of care, love, exercise, the right food and a harness that fits perfectly.

Do your employees have everything they need to do a great job?

51. Don't overload Santa's bag

Too many presents in Santa's bag can cause it to rip while they are being delivered. Imagine a rooftop covered with other children's toys. Plus it really slows Santa's schedule.

How careful are you about how your products are delivered?

52. Take time for hot chocolate

Relax with a cup of hot chocolate and a chocolate chip cookie. Use the time to remember what worked and what didn't, to enjoy what is happening now and to think about what can be done better next year.

Are you taking time for hot chocolate?

Another Word from Santa

These "secrets" may sound a lot like "Basic Marketing 101" and they are. But many people have forgotten these basics and they need to be reminded of them once again. With the advent of Facebook, Twitter, social media, email, and all the new forms of reaching out to your customers, these old basic rules still make sense:

- ✓ Take care of your customers
- ✓ Take care of your employees
- ✓ Take care of your business
- ✓ Take care of yourself.

Remember: keep the spirit of Christmas all year long and don't ever stop having fun!

I'll see you on Christmas Eve.

Your friend,

Santa